Butterfly

Susan Canizares

Scholastic Inc.

New York • Toronto • London • Auckland • Sydney

Acknowledgments

Science Consultants: Patrick R. Thomas, Ph.D., Bronx Zoo/Wildlife Conservation Park; Glenn Phillips, The New York Botanical Garden

Literacy Specialist: Ada Cordova, District 2, New York City

Design: MKR Design, Inc.

Photo Research: Barbara Scott

Endnotes: Samantha Berger

Endnote Illustrations: Craig Spearing

———————————

Photographs: Cover: Harry Rogers/Photo Researchers; p. 1: Rod Planck/NHPA; p. 2 &3: Ed Reschke/Peter Arnold; p. 4 & 5: Lior Rubin/Peter Arnold; p. 5(inset): Richard F. Trump; p. 6 & 7: Frans Lanting/Minden Pictures; p. 8,8b & 9: David Cavagnaro/DRK Photo; p. 10 & 10b: David Cavagnaro/DRK Photo; p. 11: Jeff Foott/DRK Photo; p. 12: Don Riepe/Peter Arnold.

Library of Congress Cataloging-in-Publication Data
Canizares, Susan
Butterfly / Susan Canizares.
p. cm. – (Science emergent readers)
Includes index.
Summary: Indicates the different stages in the life cycle of a butterfly.
ISBN 0-590- 76160-9 (pbk.: alk. paper)
1. Butterflies–Life cycles–Juvenile literature. [1. Butterflies–Life cycles.]
I. Title. II. Series
QL544.2.C35   1998
598.78'9–dc21   98-18819
                                                                        CIP AC

20 19 18 17 16 15 14   08   03   02   01

How do butterflies grow?

From egg

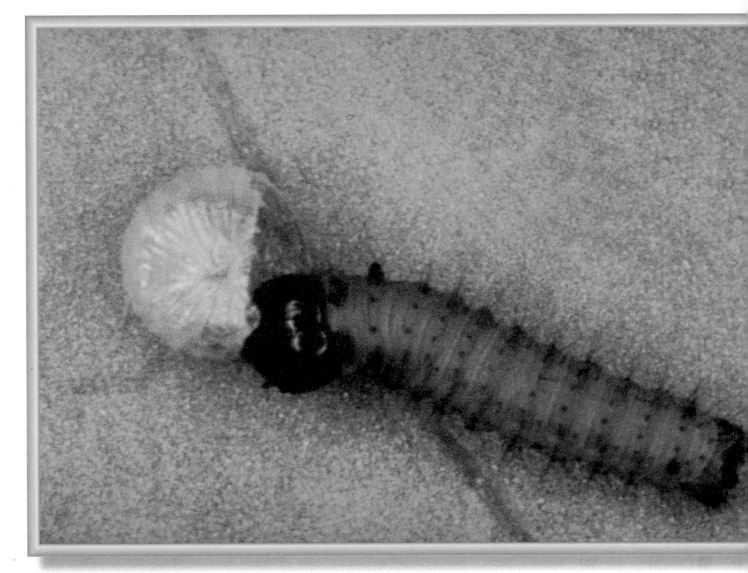

to caterpillar.

From caterpillar

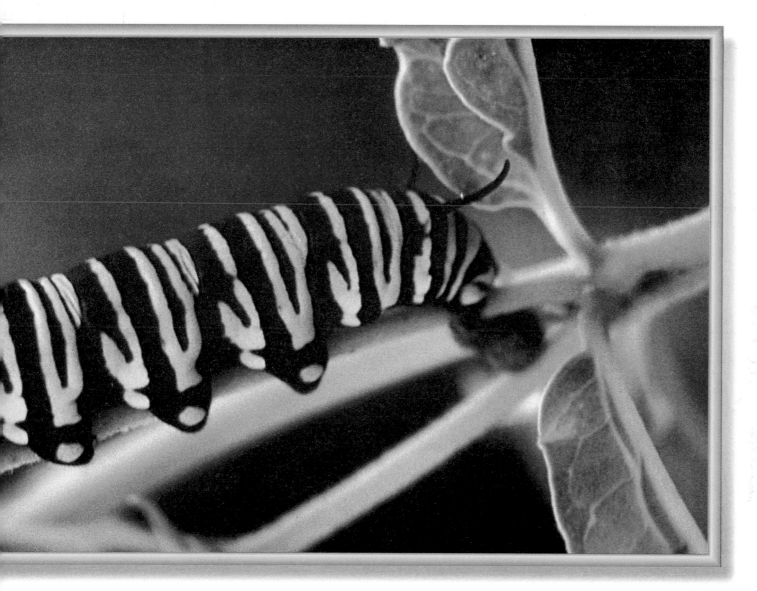

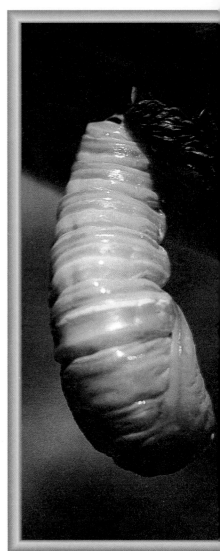

to chrysalis.

And from chrysalis

to butterfly!

Butterfly

The monarch butterfly is one of the most common butterflies in the United States. It is a good example to use to show how a butterfly grows. There are four stages in a butterfly's life. Each is radically different from the others.

Egg (pages 2–3)

The first part of a monarch butterfly's life is the egg stage. One female will lay up to 1,600 eggs in her lifetime. The eggs are laid with a covering that "glues" them to a leaf or twig. The glue hardens into a waterproof protective shell. Most butterflies lay eggs singly, but occasionally in small clusters. The eggs take anywhere from three to 12 days to hatch.

Caterpillar (pages 4–7)

The first meal of newborn baby caterpillars after hatching is their own eggshell. Next they eat the leaf the egg was on. The mother butterfly purposely lays her eggs on edible leaf sources. The young caterpillars eat almost nonstop until they are full grown. As they grow older and bigger,

they feed on chunks of leaves and plants, flower buds, and seeds. They will be full-grown caterpillars in two to four weeks. The full-grown monarch caterpillar has six eyes on each side of its head. It sees light, shade, and some move-

ment. On its lower jaw are tiny spinners used to make silk. It has three pairs of hardened legs that can hold and move food and five pairs of fleshy legs for locomotion. It will shed its skin four to six times while it's a caterpillar. This process of skin shedding is called molting.

Chrysalis (pages 8–9)

Next, the caterpillar transforms into an inactive pupa. While it is a pupa, it is gradually changing into an adult. It begins this whole process by spinning a bit of silk that it attaches to a twig or a leaf for support. It then clings to the silk thread by a sharp spine at the end of its body and molts for the last time. As the caterpillar's skin peels off, there appears a bare pupa called a chrysalis. It is an "insect in the making" and will remain enclosed in its tough flexible shell for 10 to 15 days.

Butterfly (pages 10–12)

After about two weeks in this state, a full-grown monarch butterfly emerges! The butterfly slowly opens its wet wings and fans them until they grow bigger, stronger, and fully dry. In just a few hours, the adult is ready to fly and seek a mate. Adults mate, females lay eggs, and the cycle begins again. This whole life-cycle process is called metamorphosis, which means "change of form."